Patrick J

Celtic Knots - Coloring Book For Adults

Stress Relief Coloring Book With Celtic Knot Designs

CELTIC KNOTS - COLORING BOOK FOR ADULTS

Copyright © 2018 by Patrick Brogan

Cover designed by Freepik

All rights Reserved. No part of this publication or the information in it may be quoted from or reproduced in any form by means such as printing, scanning, photocopying or otherwise without prior written permission of the copyright holder.

Disclaimer and Terms of Use: Effort has been made to ensure that the information in this book is accurate and complete, however, the author and the publisher do not warrant the accuracy of the information, text and graphics contained within the book due to the rapidly changing nature of science, research, known and unknown facts and internet.

The Author and the publisher do not hold any responsibility for errors, omissions or contrary interpretation of the subject matter herein. This book is presented solely for motivational and informational purposes only.

#1

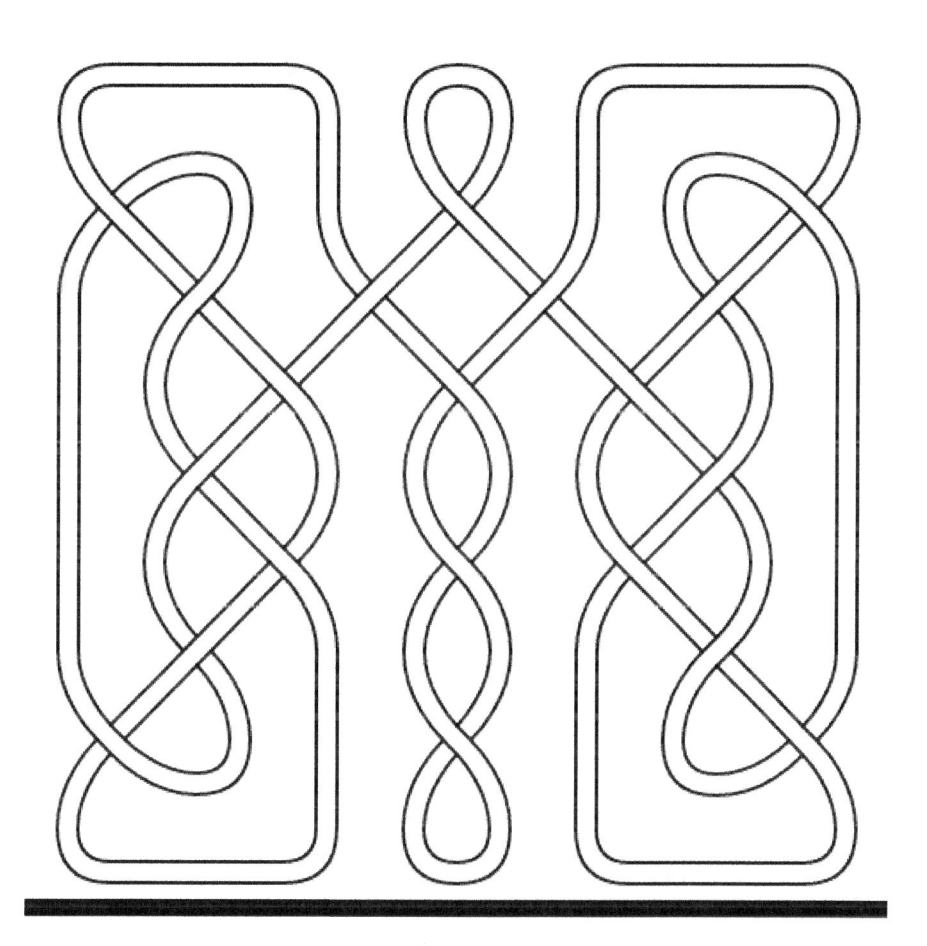

#2

#3

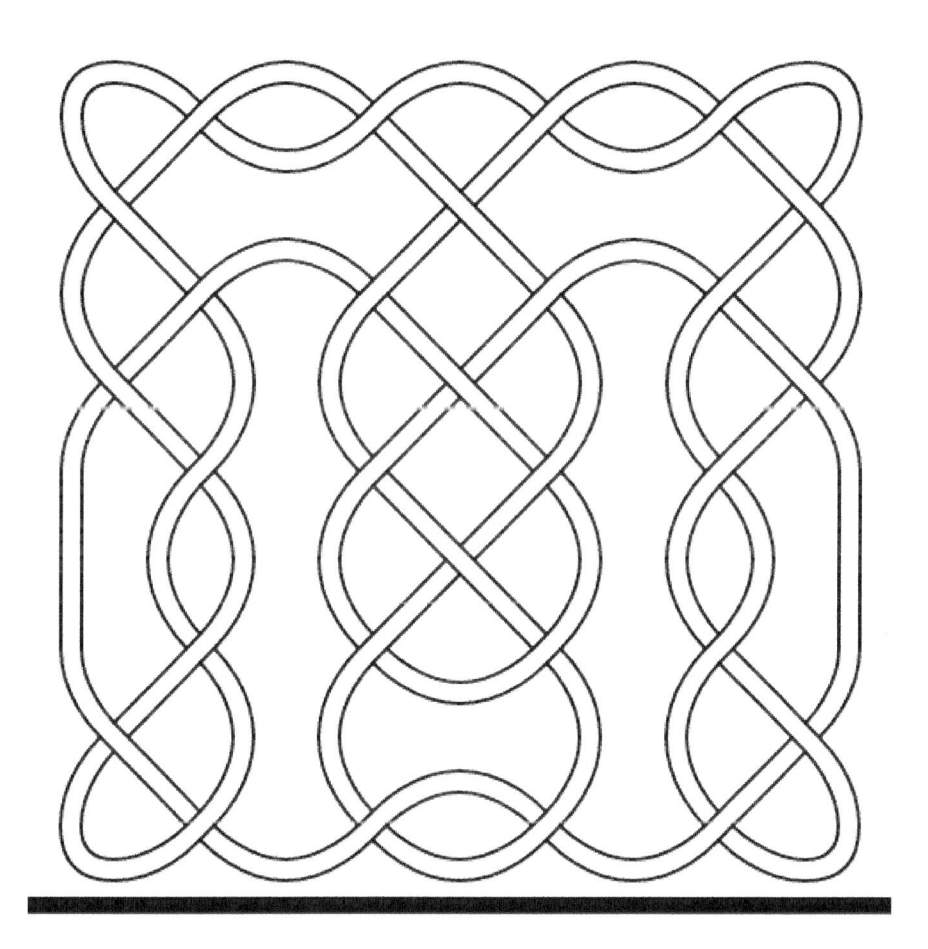

#4

#5

#6

#7

#8

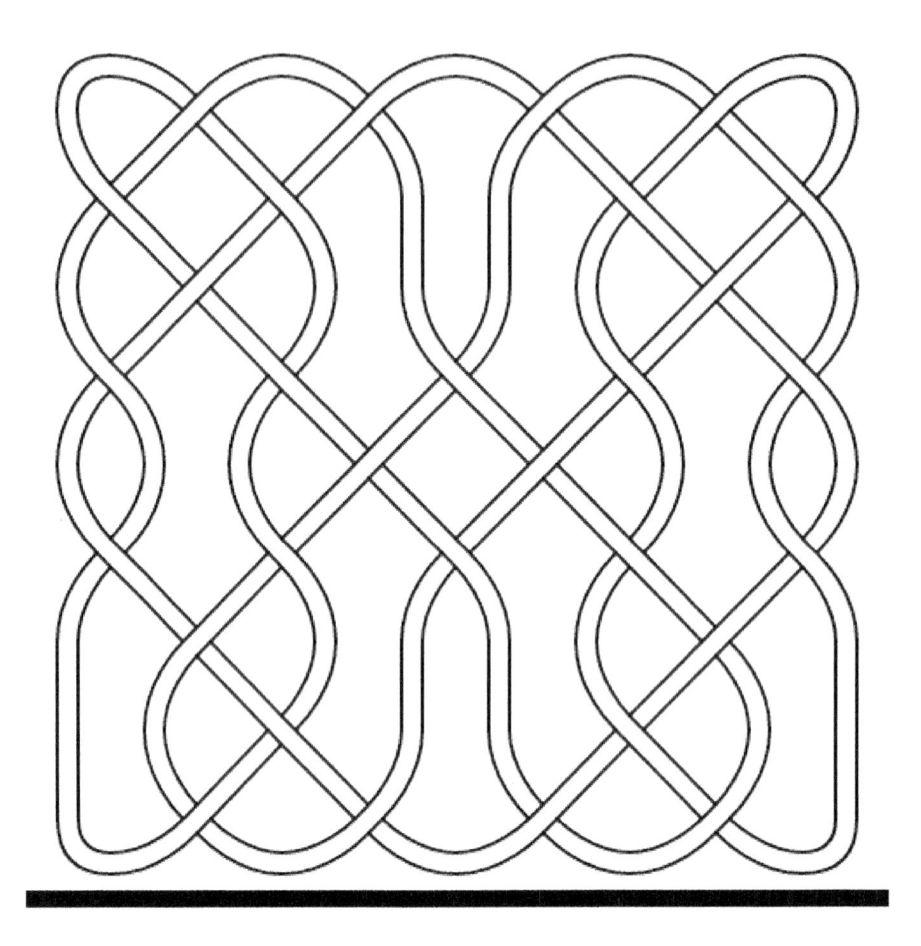

#9

#10

12

#11

#12

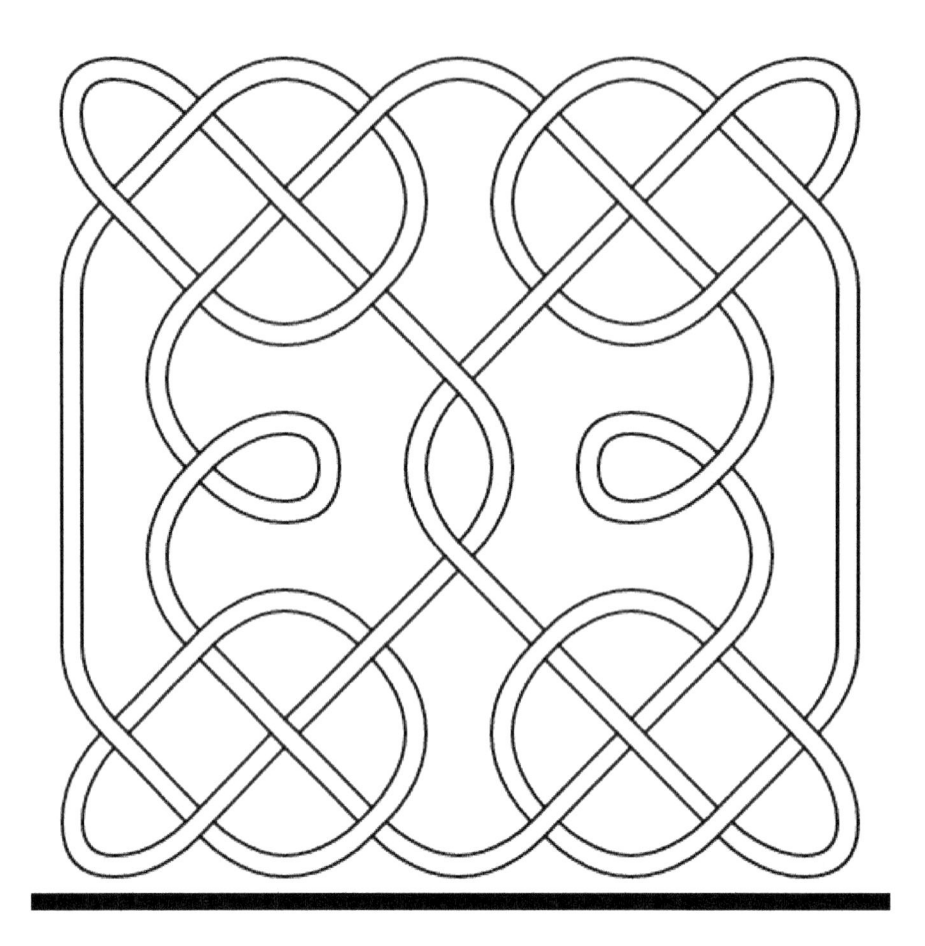

#13

#14

#15

#16

#17

#18

#19

#20

22

#21

#22

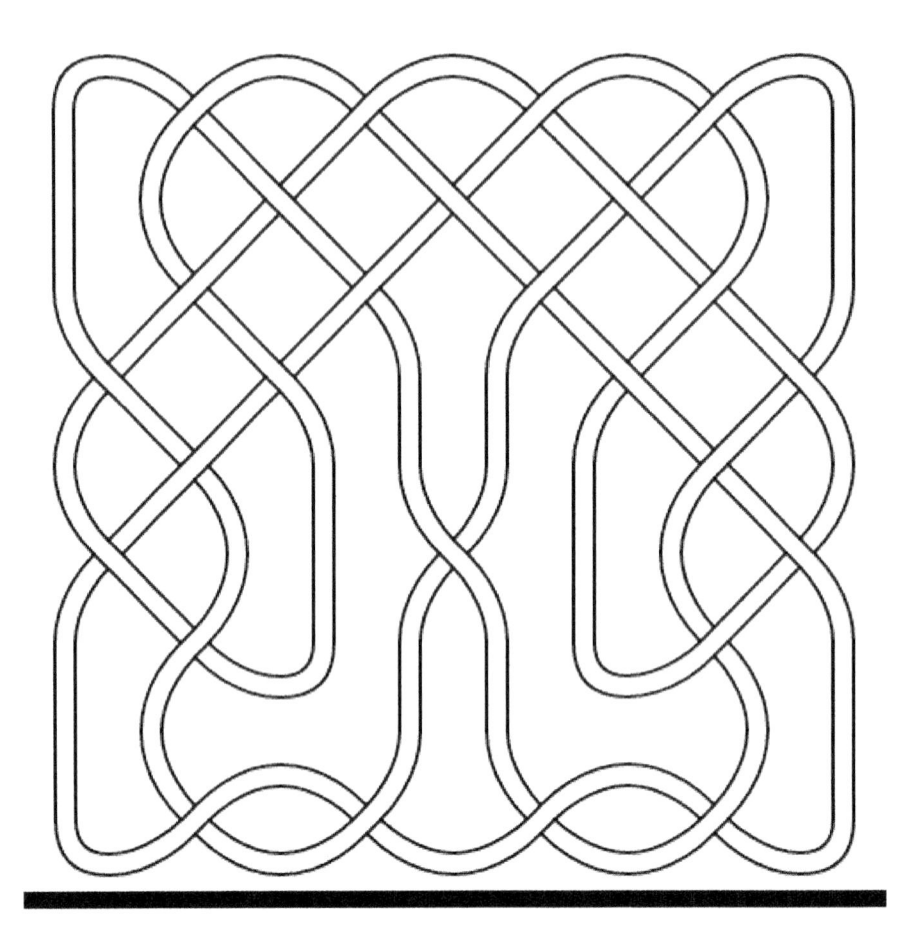

#23

#24

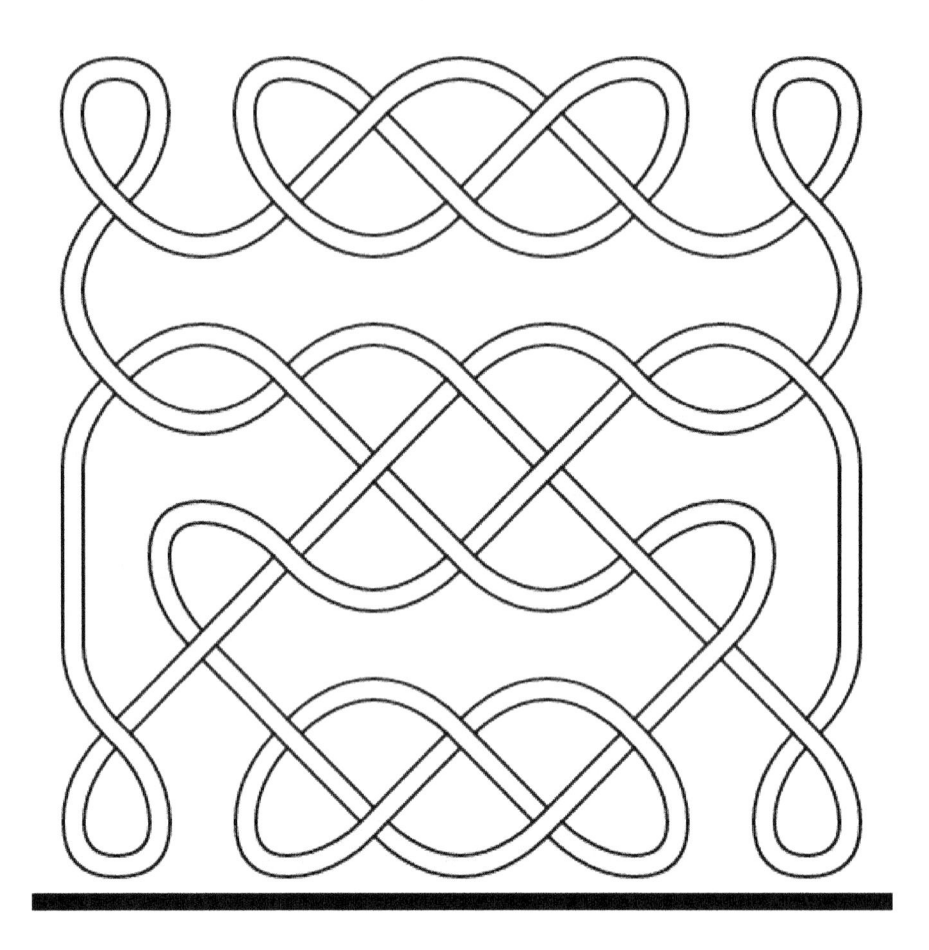

#25

#26

#27

#28

#29

#30

#31

#32

#33

#34

#35

#36

#37

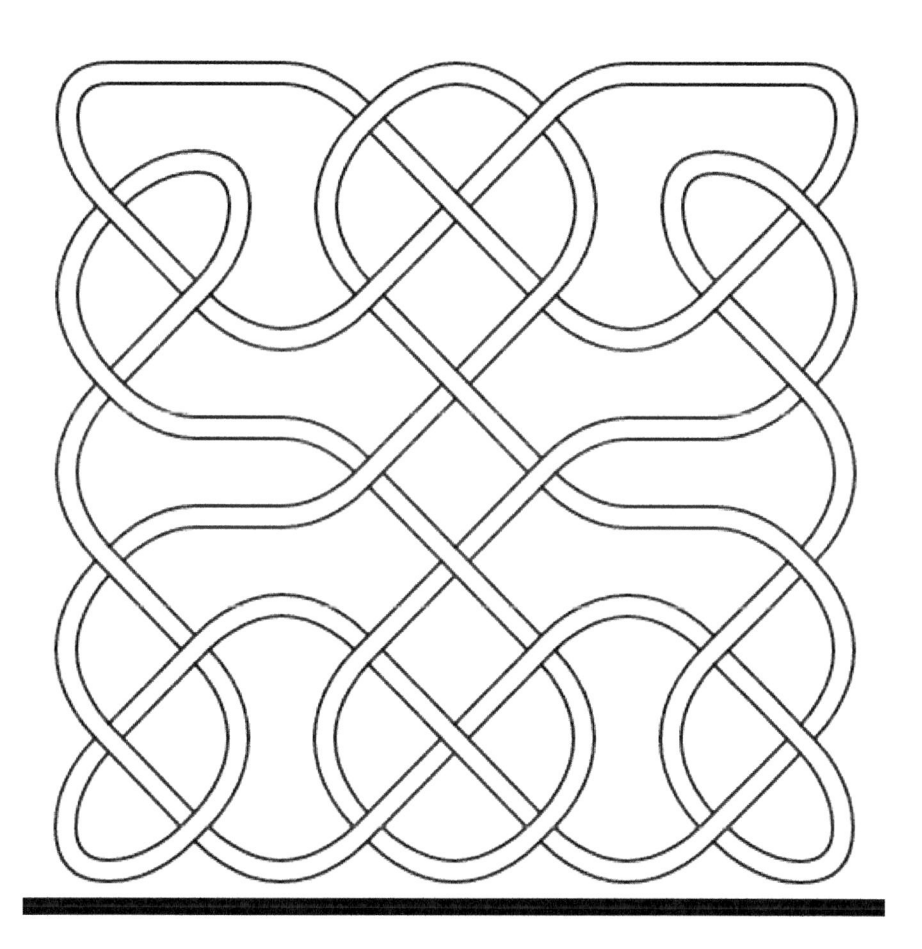

#38

#39

#40

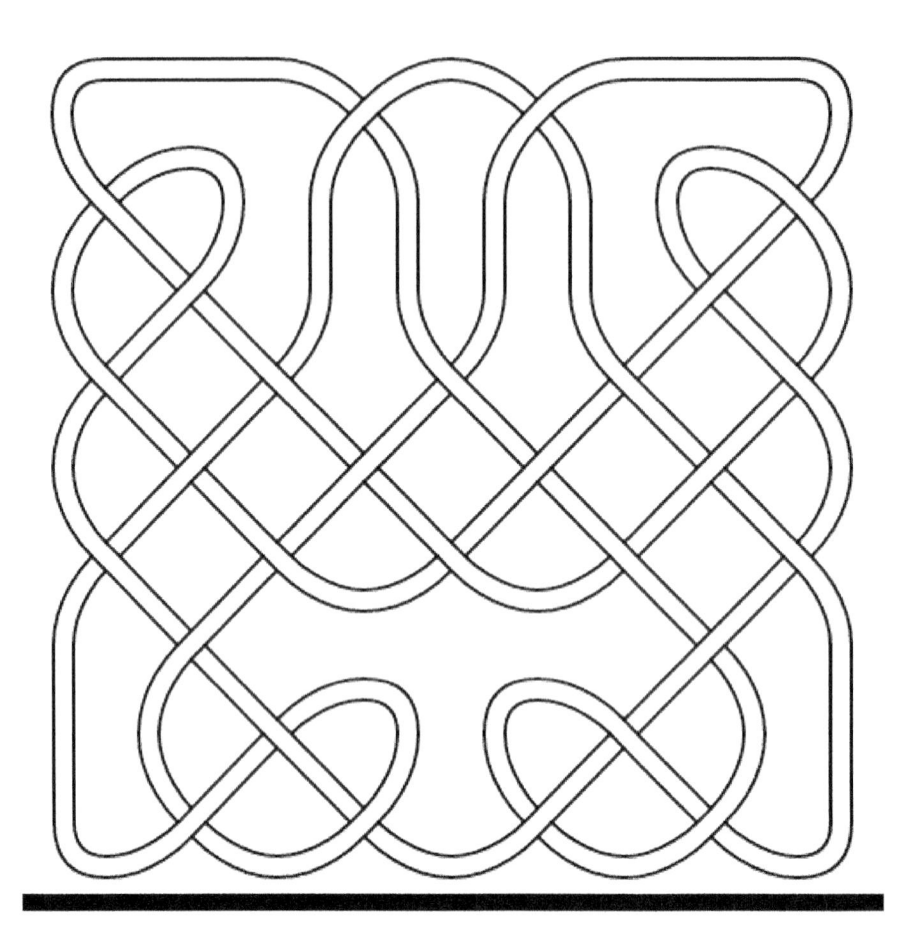

#41

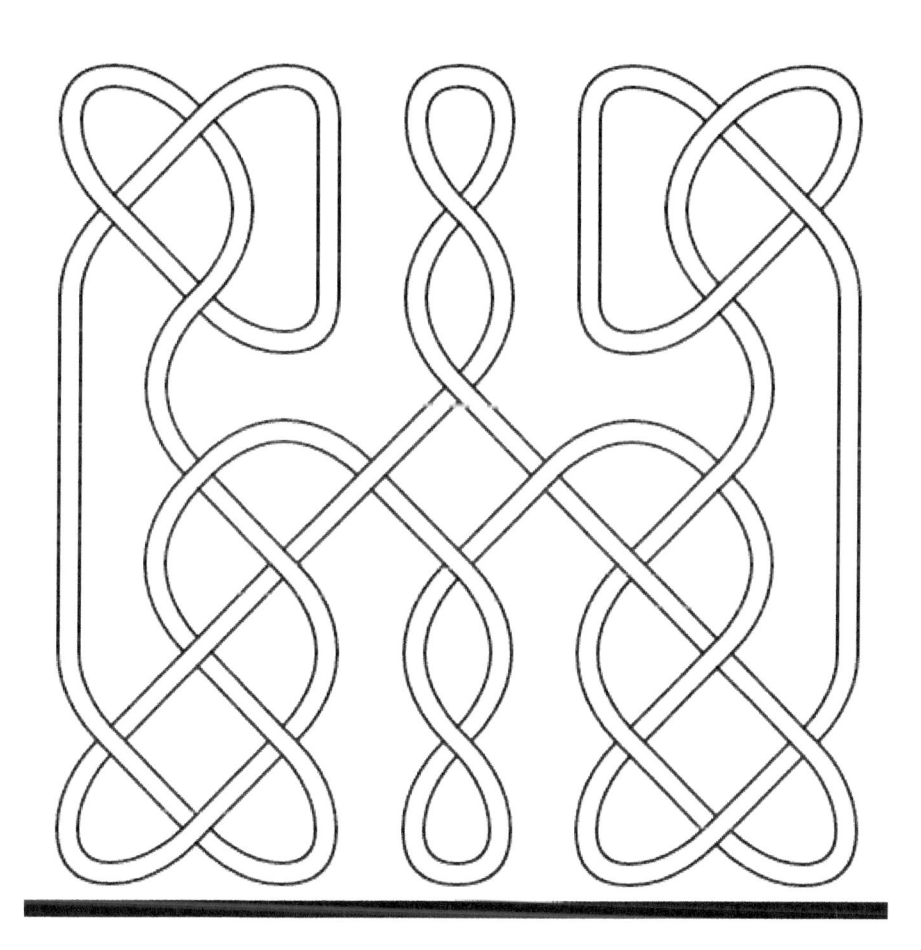

#42

#43

#44

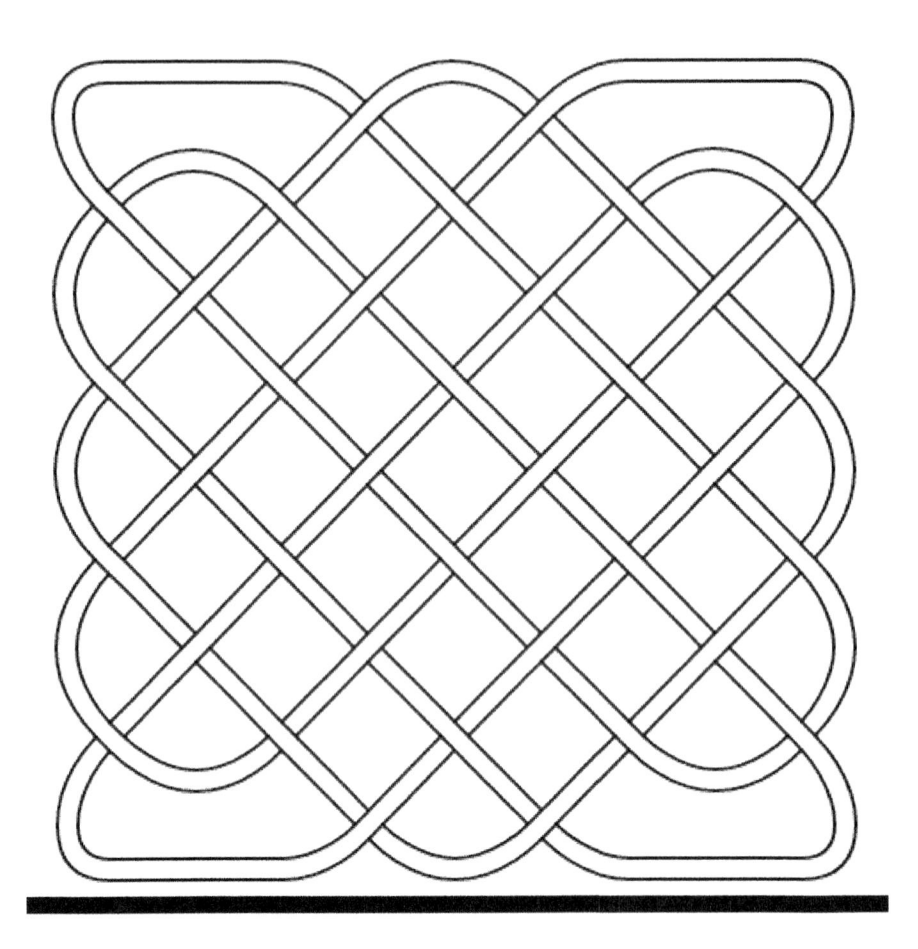

#45

#46

#47

#48

#49

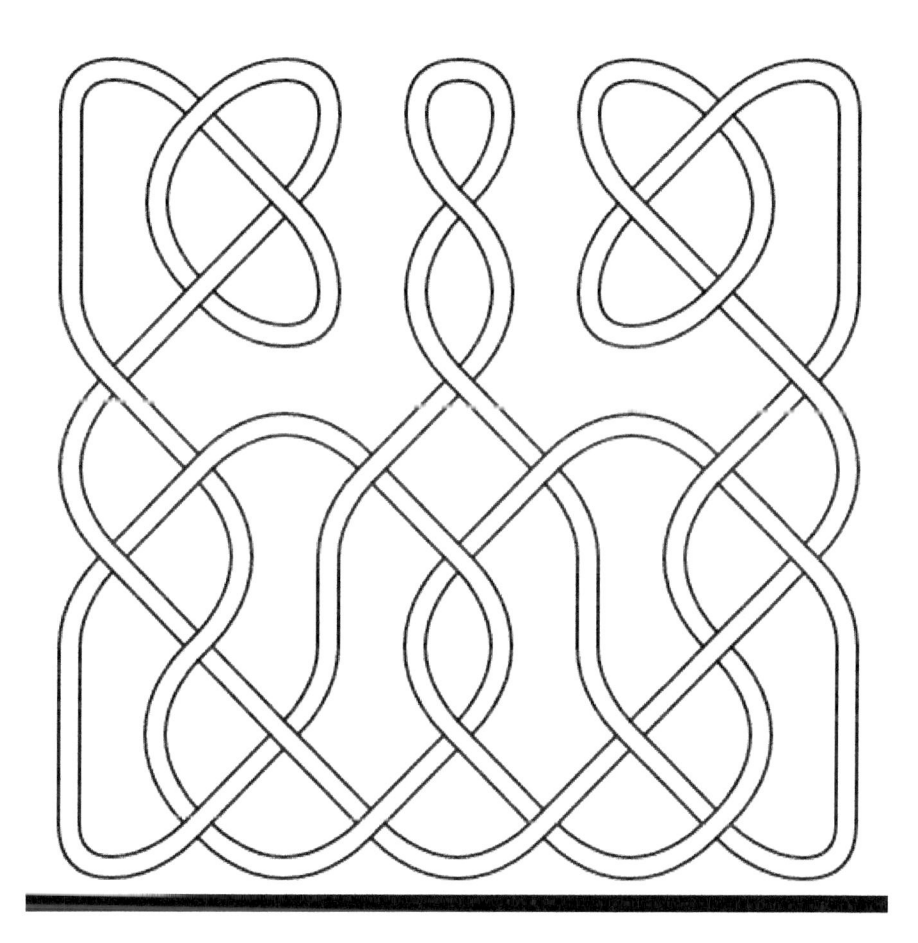

#50

#51

#52

#53

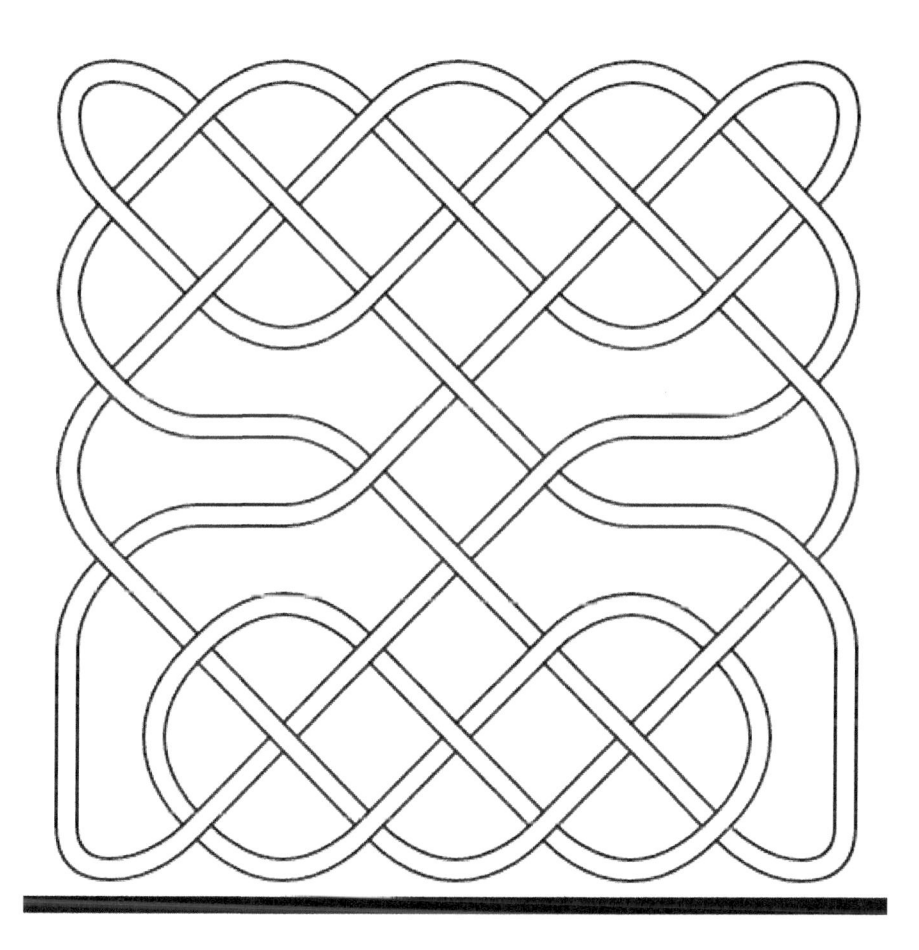

#54

#55

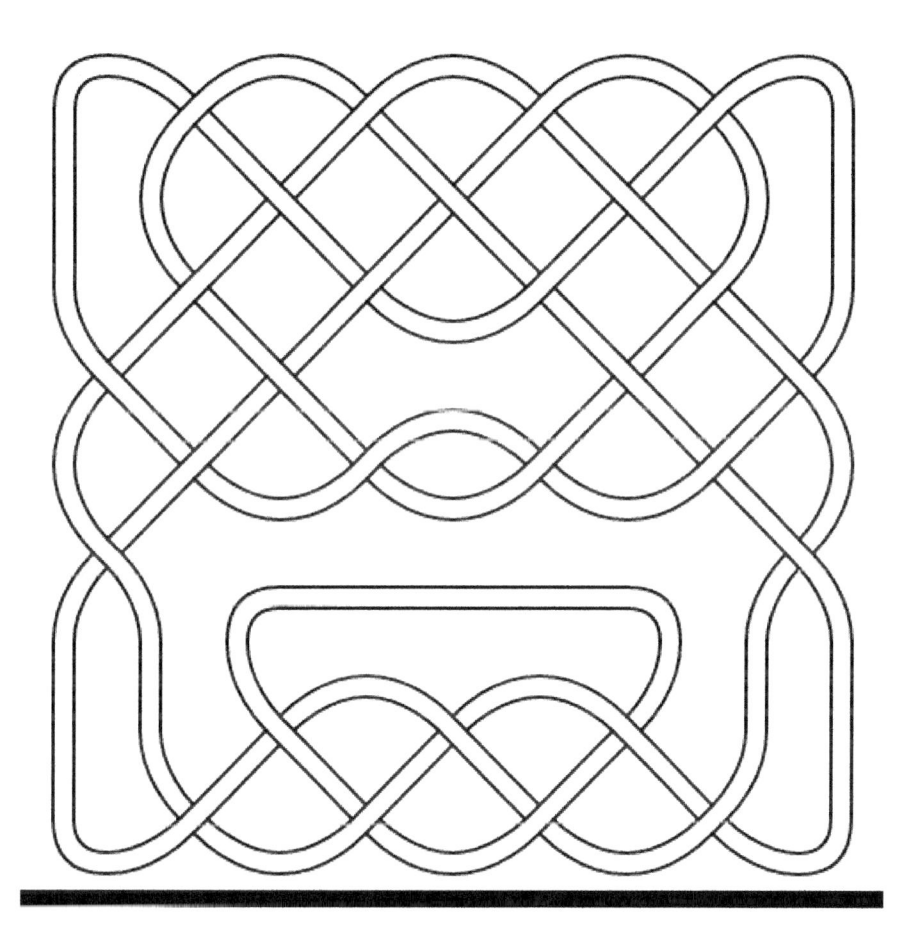

#56

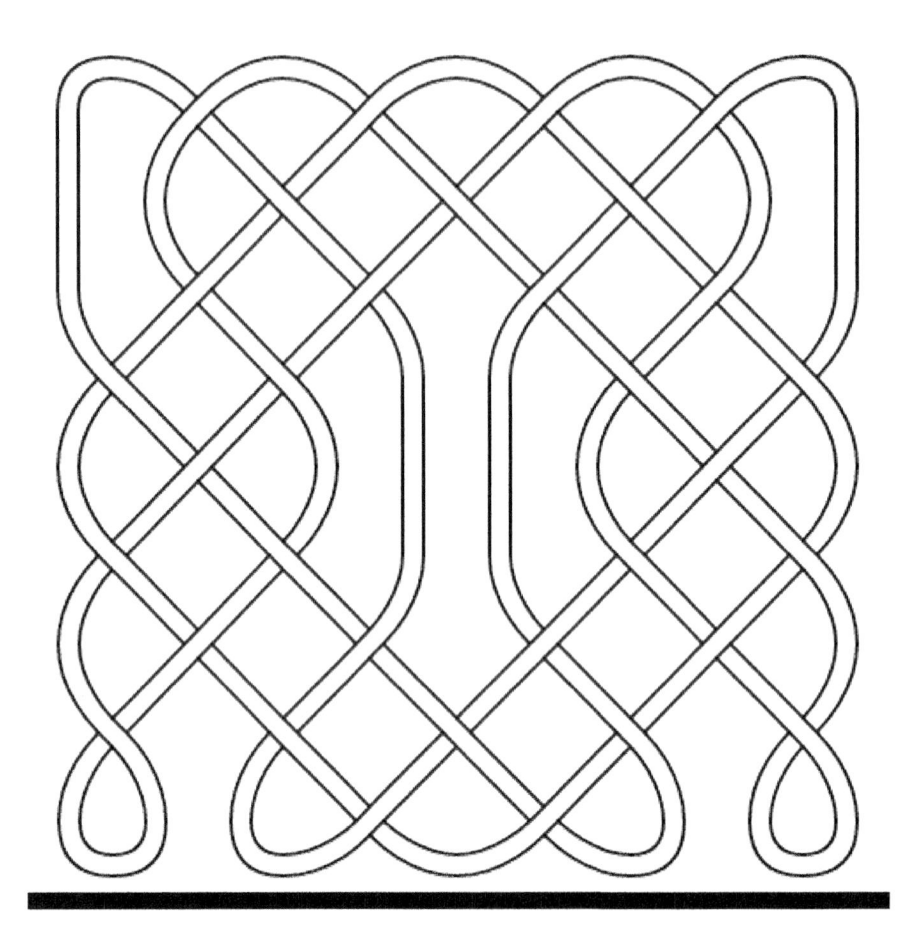

58

#57

#58

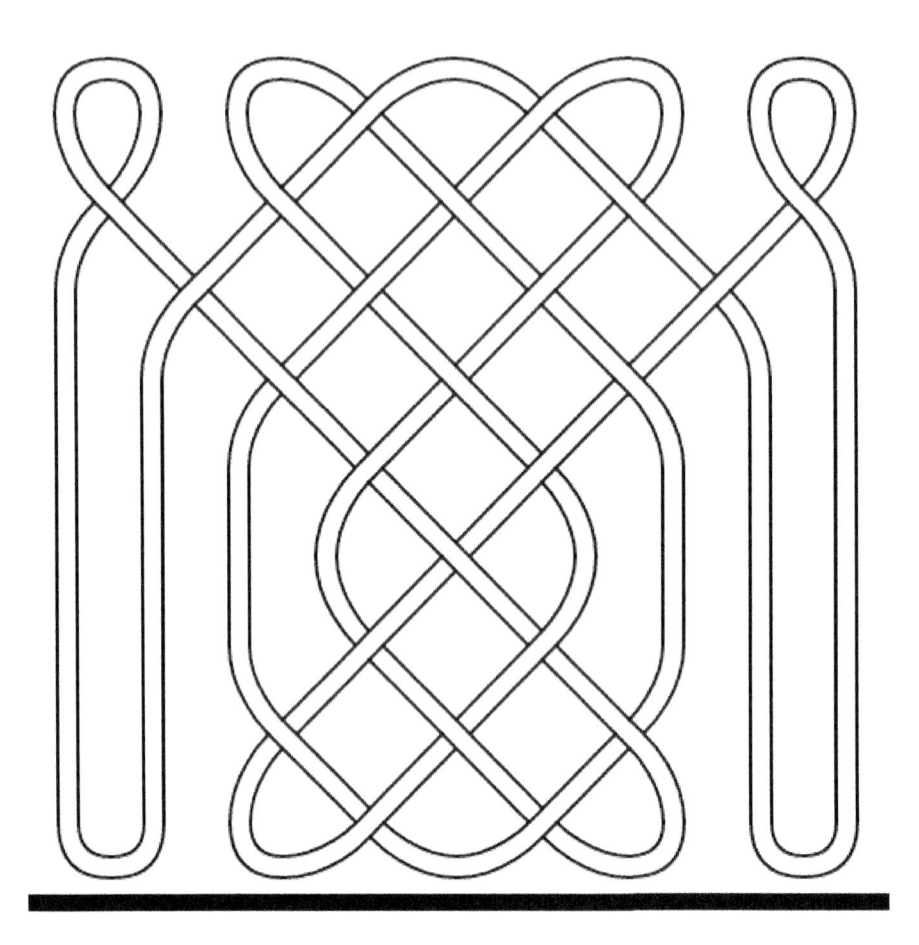

#59

#60

#61

#62

#63

#64

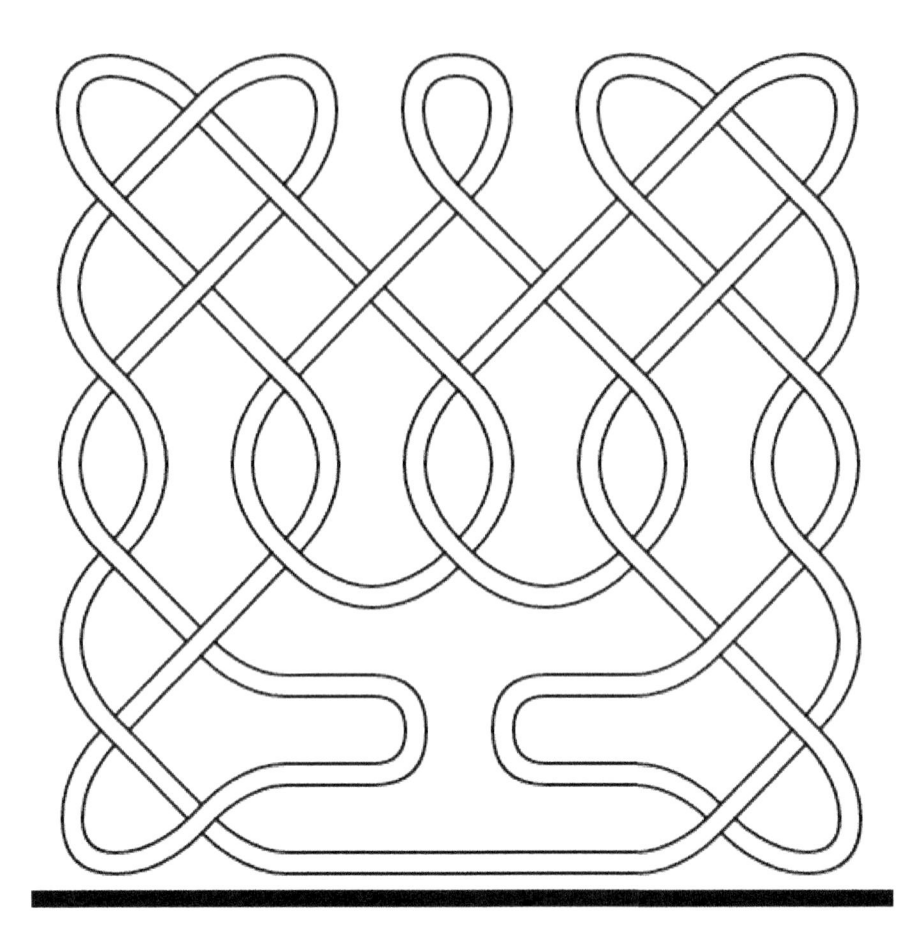

#65

#66

#67

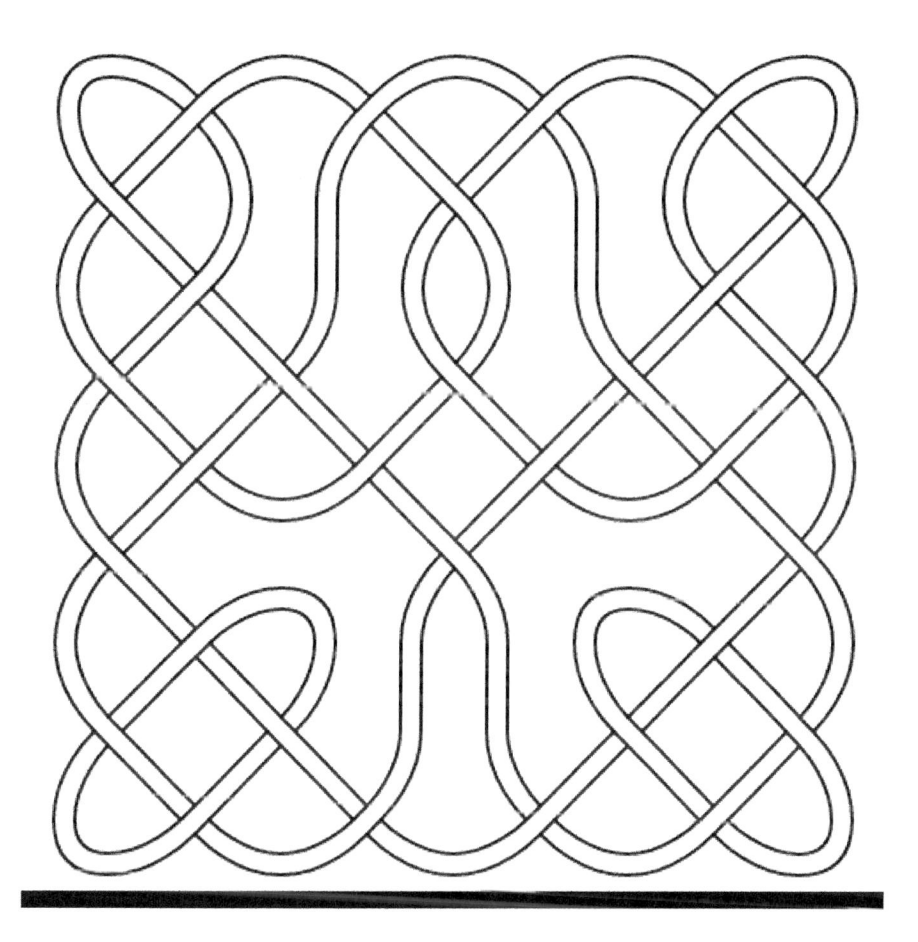

#68

#69

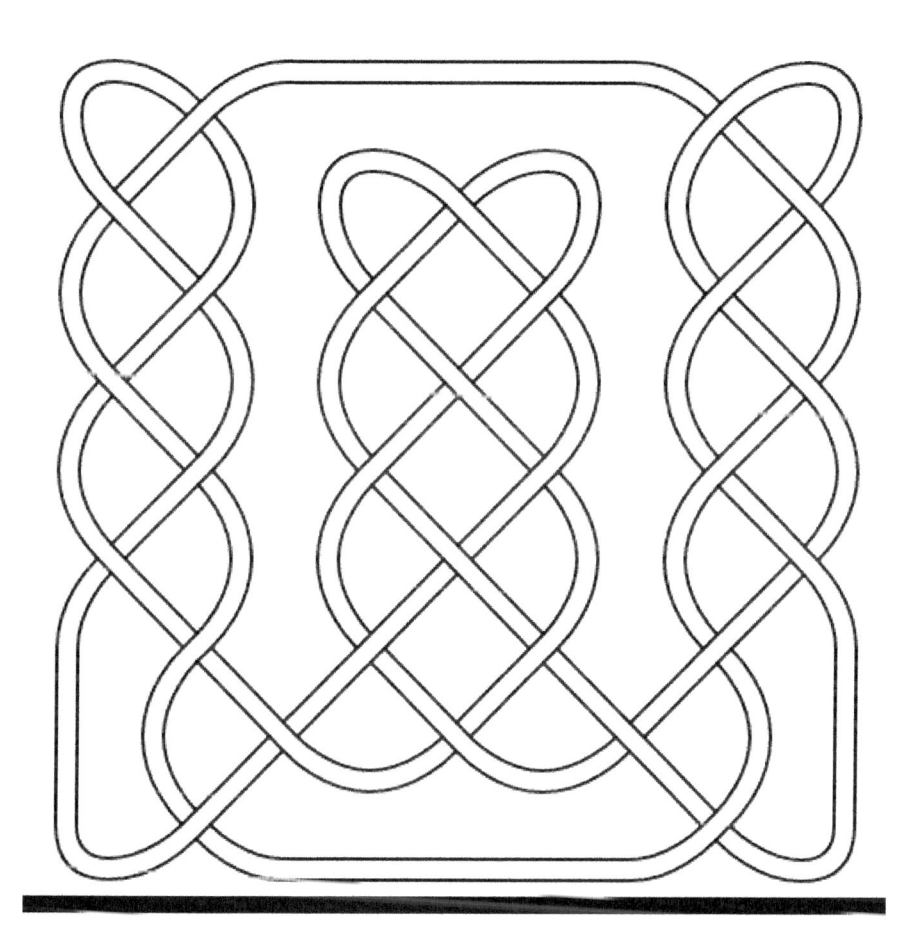

#70

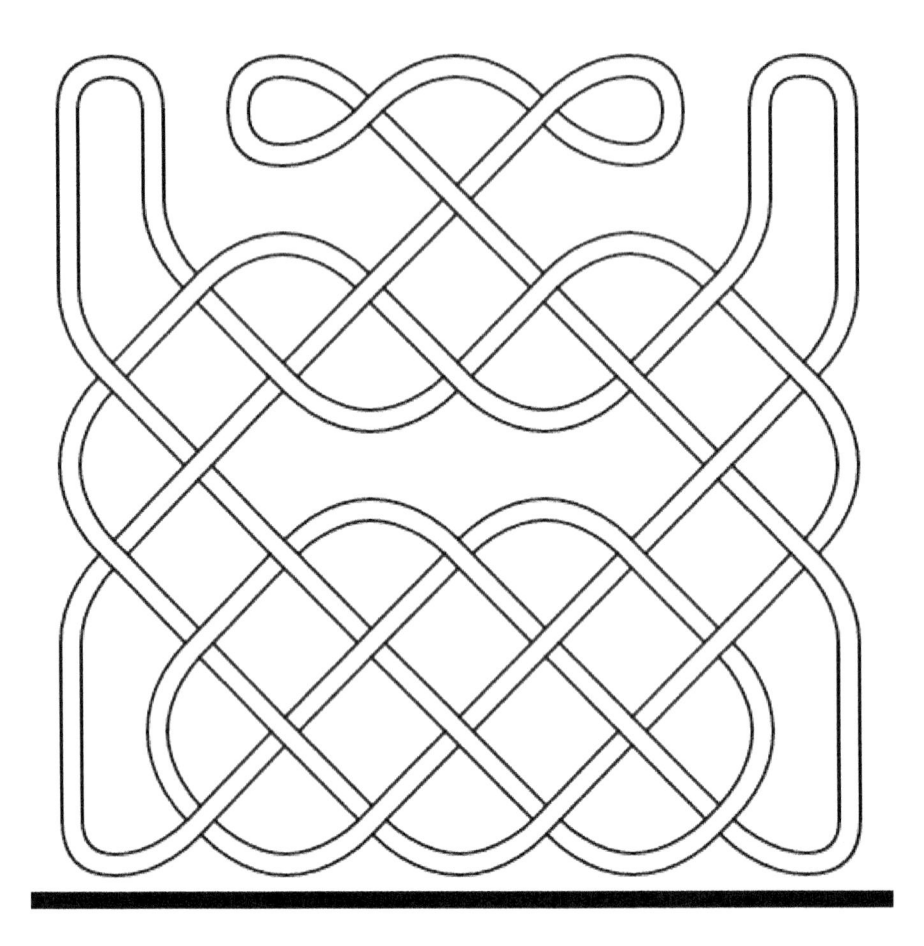

#71

#72

#73

#74

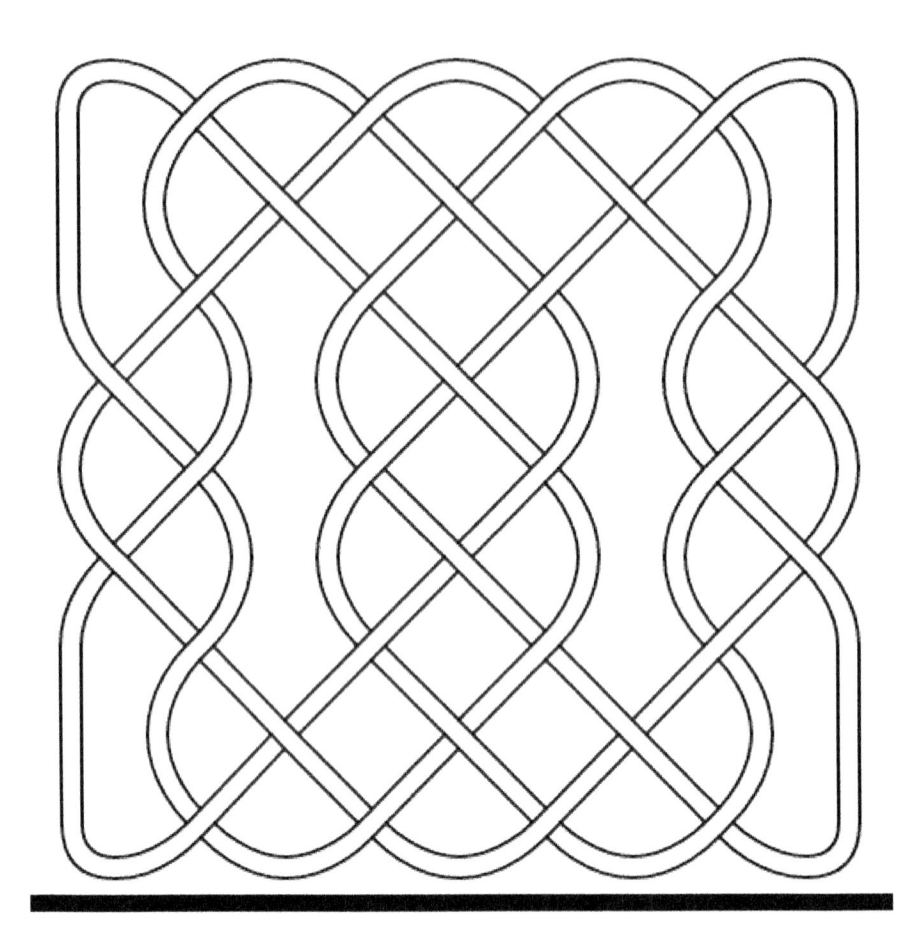

#75

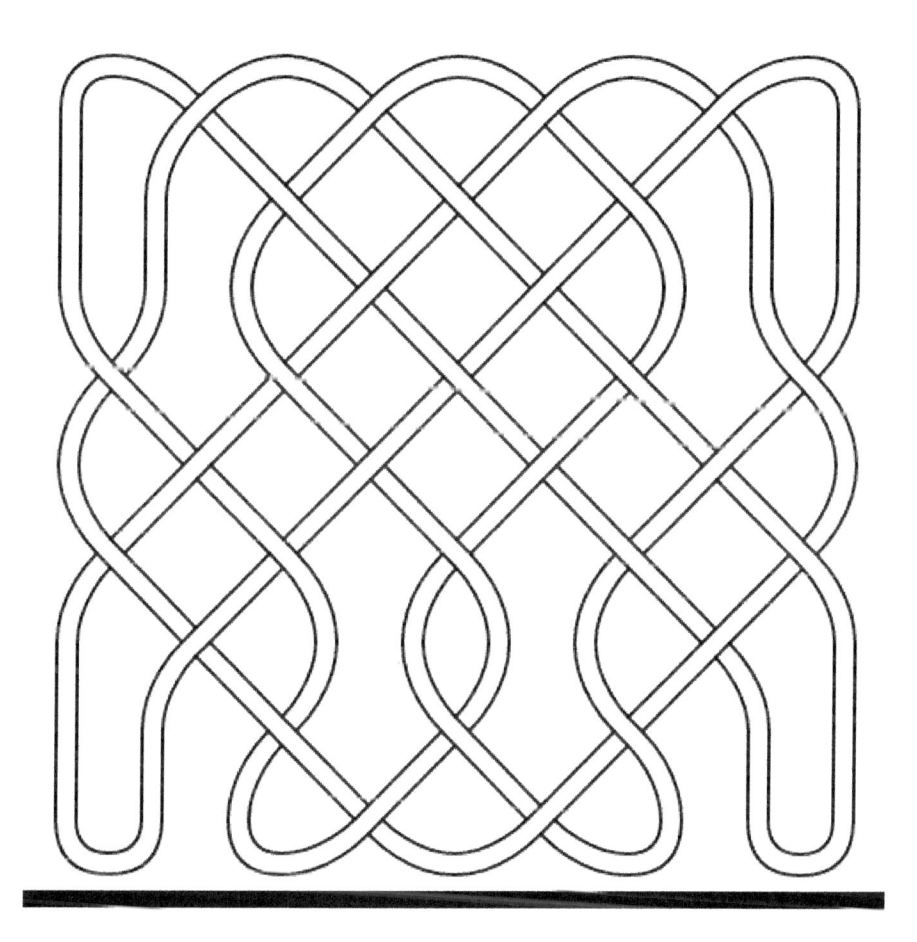

#76

#77

#78

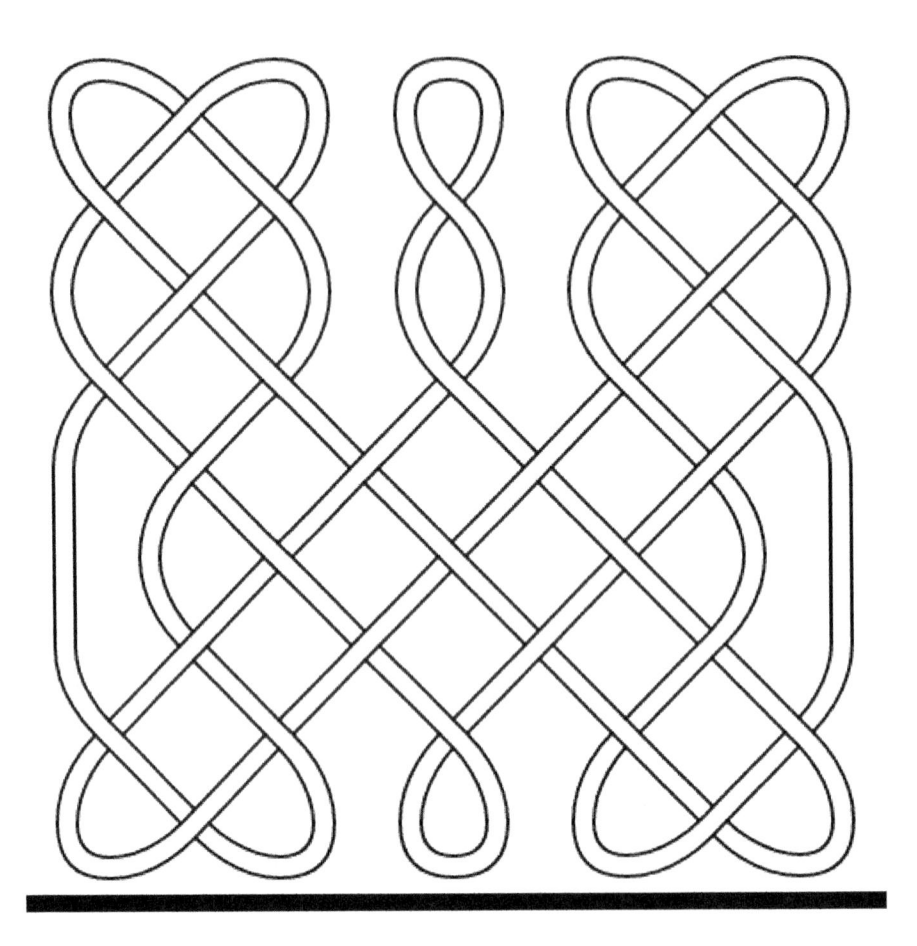

#79

#80

#81

#82

#83

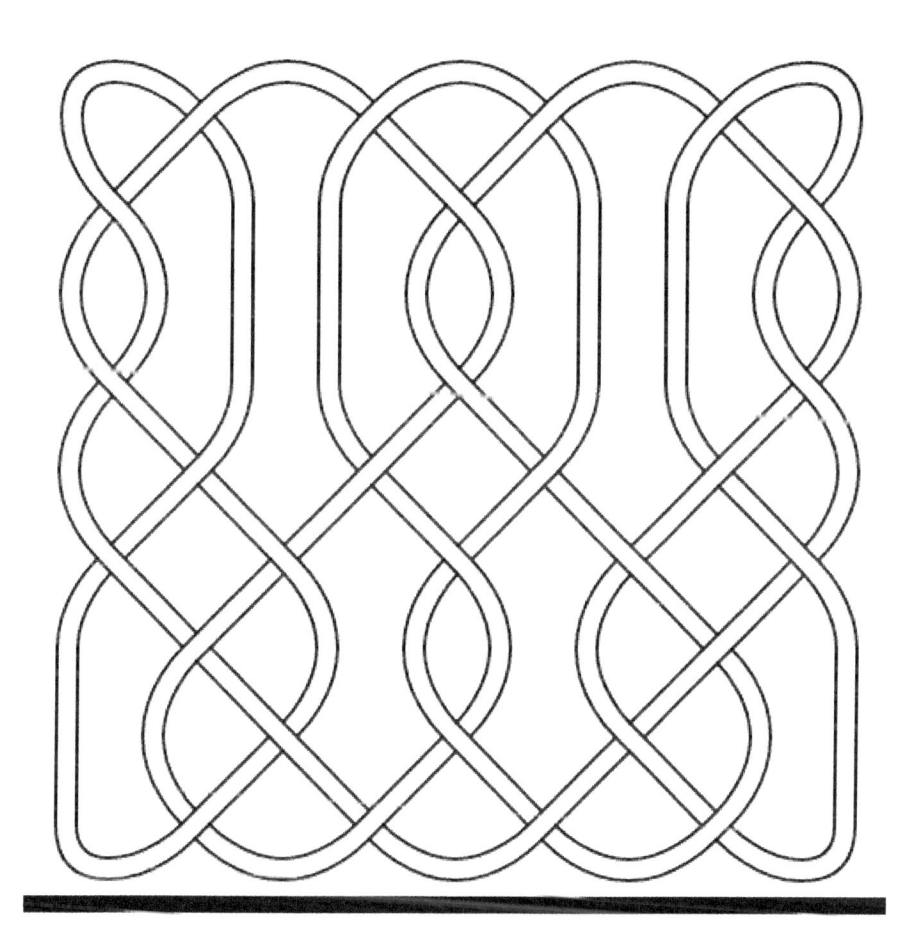

#84

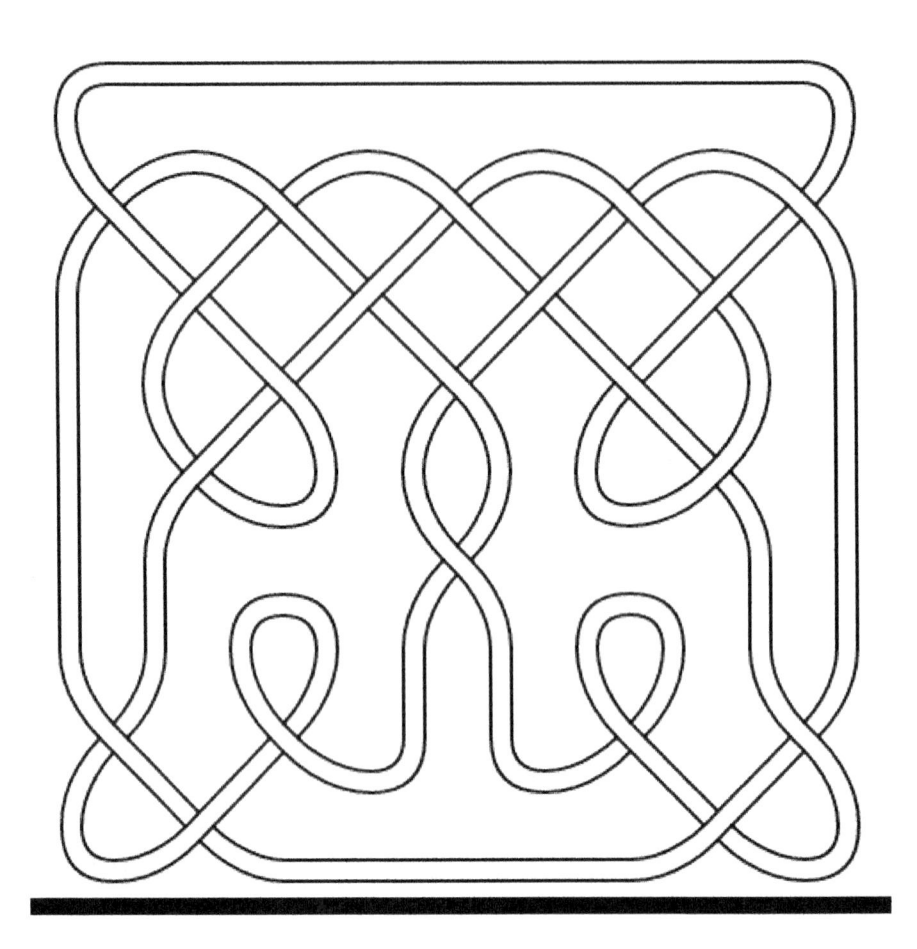

86

#85

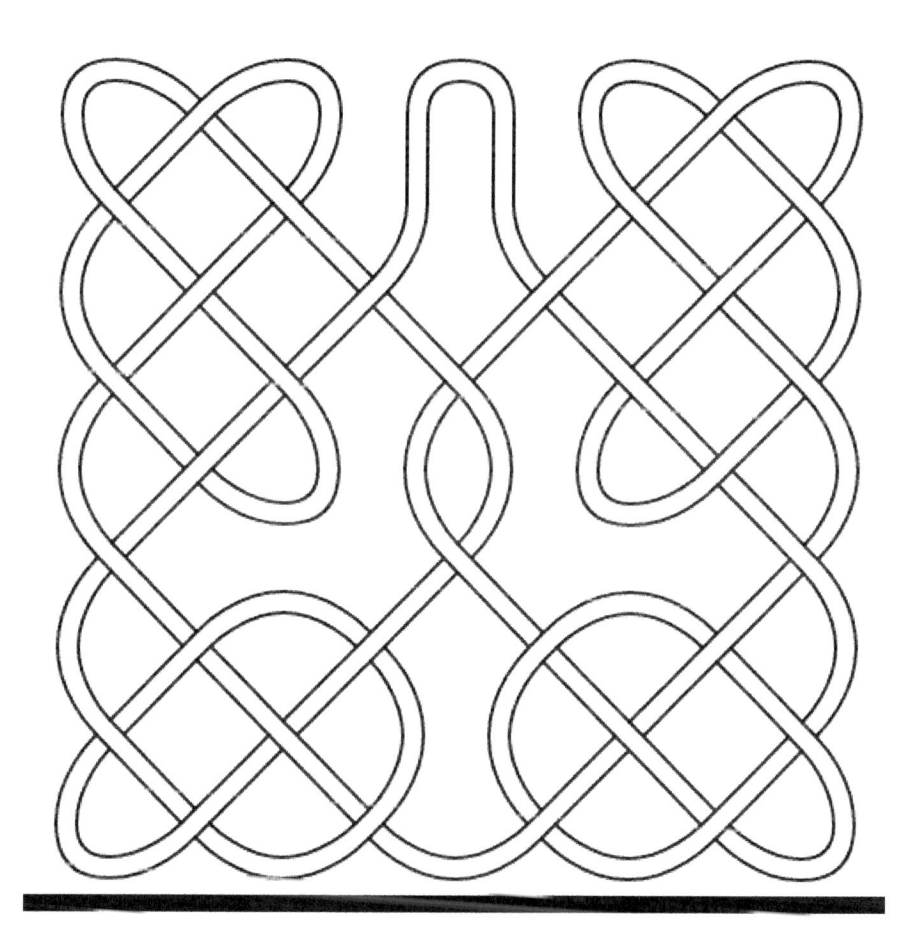

#86

#87

#88

#89

#90

#91

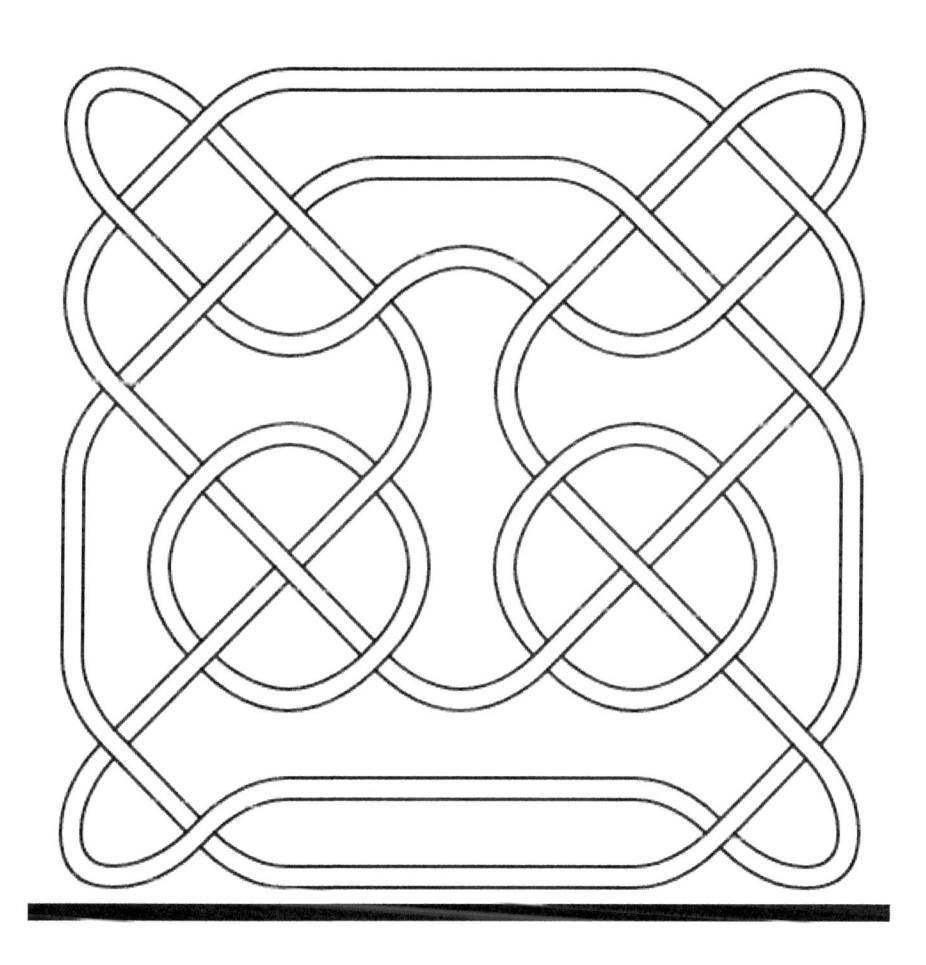

#92

#93

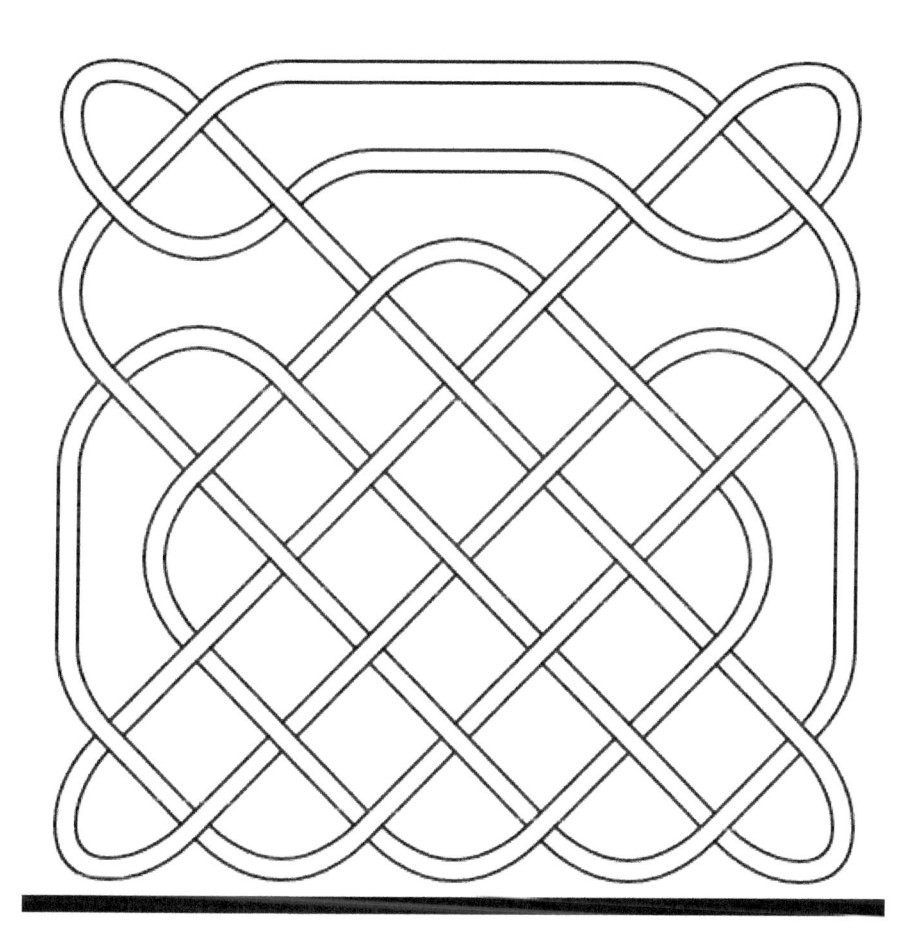

#94

#95

#96

#97

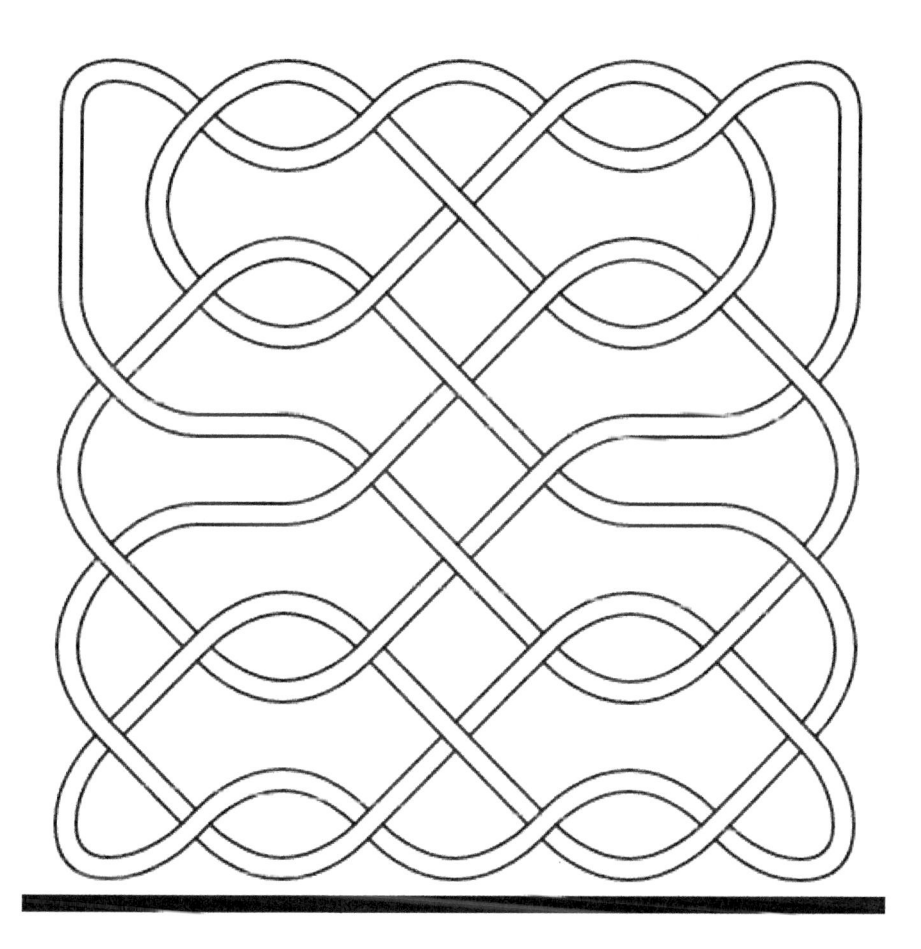

#98

#99

#100

Printed in Dunstable, United Kingdom